THIRTY MINUTES OVER OREGON

A JAPANESE PILOT'S WORLD WAR II STORY

by **Marc Tyler Nobleman**

Illustrated by **Melissa Iwai**

Clarion Books

HOUGHTON MIFFLIN HARCOURT | Boston • New York

To Daniela. I wouldn't know Nobuo if not for you. —M.T.N.

For Denis and Jamie. —M.I.

ACKNOWLEDGMENTS

In broad ways, a book is like a war: both leave you changed. . . and both are group efforts. Thank you again to Bill McCash (research MVP), Didi Sager (for passing along the obituary), the mock cover artists—professional (Tim Bush, Ralph Cosentino, Justin LaRocca Hansen, Kevin O'Malley, Mike Rex, Julia Sarcone-Roach, Brad Sneed), the mock cover artists— youth (Alex Claypool, Alex Dragunoff, Tommy Flood, Coby Resnick), Brenda Jacques, Susana Fernandez, Lori Steele, W. Garth Dowling, Mark Mead, Glenn Woodfin, Mike Moran, Lisa Phelps, Sarah Cortell, Robyn Soiseth Choffel, Fumihiro Fujita, Tatsuo Motegi, Harehiko Nomura, Ilana Sol, Candy Fleming (for referring me to Jennifer Greene), Audrey Vernick (ditto), Jennifer Berne, Susan Goodman, Katie Davis, Donna Bowman Bratton, Greg Pincus, Julie Danielson, Betsy Bird, Travis Jonker, Caryn Wiseman, Emily van Beek, and especially Jennifer Greene.

Clarion Books
3 Park Avenue, New York, New York 10016

Clarion Books is an imprint of
Houghton Mifflin Harcourt Publishing Company.

hmhco.com

The illustrations in this book were executed in watercolor and mixed media. The text was set in Farnham Display.

Library of Congress Cataloging-in-Publication Data is available.
ISBN 978-0-544-43076-1

Manufactured in China
SCP 10 9 8 7 6 5
4500817828

Prologue

On December 7, 1941, the Japanese bombed Pearl Harbor, an American naval base on Hawaii. The surprise attack killed thousands of soldiers and brought America into World War II.

To retaliate, the US bombed Tokyo from the sky. This became known as the Doolittle Raid, which would later be memorialized in both a book and film called *Thirty Seconds Over Tokyo*. In response, Japan set out to prove that continental America—though far from all World War II combat—could also be bombed.

This is the story of what happened next.

宣戰を布告

八萬二年　(大曜日)　新聞　立行

Star-Bulletin

Associated Press by Transpacific

SAN FRANCISCO, Dec. 7.—President Roosevelt announced this morning that Japanese planes had attacked Manila and Pearl Harbor.

WAR!
U BOMBED BY

FOUNDED IN 1867
NNEAPOLIS, MINN, SATURDAY, APRIL 18

Fifteen miles off the Oregon coast, on September 9, 1942, Nobuo Fujita strode across the slippery deck of a submarine.

He gripped the 400-year-old samurai sword that had been in his family for generations. "Come on," he told his navigator. "It will soon be sunup." They climbed into a small plane that was about to be launched—by catapult—toward the United States.

NOBUO FUJITA

1942

As he did before every flight, Nobuo strapped the sword to his seat for luck. Crew members loaded 168-pound bombs under each wing of the plane. The Japanese hoped that the bombs would start a fire that would consume the Oregon woods, then rage into nearby towns and cities.

"Do not tell anyone," Nobuo's commander had told him, "not even your wife." So instead of sharing with Ayako what Japan had entrusted him to do, Nobuo left strands of hair and fingernail clippings for her to bury if he didn't make it back. If the American military shot at him, his plane would not be fast enough to evade being hit.

The catapult flung the plane off the sub with a hard *whoosh*.

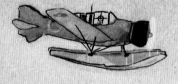

Steering into the rising sun, Nobuo scanned
the sky for American fighters but saw none.

When he flew over the tiny town of Brookings, Oregon, some of the residents heard the motor. A few saw the plane puttering through the fog. But almost none suspected it was an enemy aircraft.

Shortly after 6:00 a.m., high above the thickly wooded mountains nine miles east of Brookings, Nobuo gave his navigator the order: "The bombs are to be dropped here."

Nobuo wheeled the plane. Over his shoulder, he caught sight of a white flash below. He beelined back to the ocean, flying low enough to clip treetops.

He landed on the water, and the sub crew hoisted the plane aboard with a crane. They quickly removed the wings and floats and stowed everything in a watertight hangar.

The sub then dove 250 feet.

Meanwhile, the forest was burning . . . a bit. Only one of the two bombs had exploded, sparking patches of fire that didn't spread. The ground was too damp from recent rain. The other bomb had buried itself on impact without a trace.

Four men from forest lookout stations spotted smoke and trudged several hours to the remote site and extinguished the flames. They figured the fire was caused by lightning. But they noticed a splintered tree and, beneath it, a small pit in a circle of scorched earth. Widening the pit into a crater, they uncovered metal fragments. Some had markings—in Japanese.

The news that a foreign foe had flown in and out of American airspace undetected zipped through Brookings. Townsfolk were shaken, but many were more concerned for their relatives fighting overseas. Several newspapers put forth the notion that the plane may have taken off from a sub, but this was dismissed as improbable. The military assumed that the incident was isolated and did little to increase their efforts to defend the coast.

Twenty days after the bombing, Nobuo did it again. Same plan, same plane.

Only that time, for greater stealth, he went by night. To protect coastal communities from becoming easy targets, the US military routinely ordered blackouts during the war. But the lighthouse at Cape Blanco remained lit, and guided to shore by its beam, Nobuo headed to a wooded area north of Brookings and dropped two more bombs on Oregon.

On his return, Nobuo could not locate the sub. Nearly out of fuel, he resigned himself to dying with honor by winging back and crashing into the lighthouse. "The mission comes first, the sub next," he said to his navigator. "We come last."

But a moment later, he glimpsed a dark, snaky shimmer on the ocean swells . . . an oil leak from his sub.

The Japanese believed the second two bombs had detonated. Americans scoured the woods but found no fragments and no damage—or if they did, they kept quiet about it. Either way, Japan claimed both invasions as victories. They had caught America off-guard.

After years at war, Nobuo returned to Japan, anxious to rejoin Ayako and their young son and daughter, Yoshi and Yoriko. As his ship pulled into port—into home—Nobuo gazed through binoculars to mask his tears.

In 1945, Japan surrendered to the United States and its allies, ending World War II.

Nobuo opened a hardware store and lived quietly in a Tokyo suburb. He never discussed his Oregon raids, though they were rarely out of his mind. And the residents of Brookings largely forgot about their close call—until 1962.

That year, the Brookings Jaycees, a leadership organization, was looking for a way to boost tourism to their sleepy burg. One member had a bold idea. He suggested that they track down the Japanese bomber pilot and invite him to attend their annual Memorial Day festival as a guest of honor. So they did.

To their surprise, Nobuo accepted their invitation.

And they weren't the only ones who were shocked—this was the first
Nobuo's family had heard of what he had done in America.

One US newspaper published a petition condemning the idea. Those who signed felt that any soldier saluted in Brookings should be American. Furthermore, it would be expensive to fly over Nobuo, Ayako, and Yoshi, now 26, who would act as translator.

Despite the pressure to cancel the visit, the Jaycees didn't give in. Welcoming Nobuo, they announced, would be a symbol of reconciliation not just between individuals but between nations.

Another newspaper printed a letter from a veteran who wrote, "He was doing a job and we were doing a job." Other veterans—including the governor of Oregon and President John F. Kennedy—also praised the invitation. Protesters began to open their minds.

Yet Nobuo was nervous. Initially he had feared that Americans were tricking him into coming so they could put him on trial as a war criminal. He worried that they would insult him, egg him, beat him. But he knew he had to go, no matter what. "It would be impolite to refuse," he said.

Again, he brought his family sword. This time, however, it was not for luck.

Over the years, Nobuo's war pride had shriveled into guilt. His brother had been lost in battle. His country had suffered catastrophically when the United States dropped atomic bombs on the cities of Hiroshima and Nagasaki. And though *his* bombings hadn't hurt anyone, that had been the intention.

If the people of Brookings accepted the apology he planned, he would gift the sword to the town. If they did not, he would use the sword to commit *seppuku*, traditional Japanese suicide by a person overcome with shame.

A large group of people awaited his arrival at the airport. To his relief, they greeted him and his family not with anger, but with warmth.

Gesturing to the jetliner he'd flown in, Nobuo said in good spirit, "A little larger than the plane in which I made my first trip."

During the festival parade, an official introduced the Fujitas, who bowed three times to the applauding crowd.

Nobuo shook the hand of a six-year-old boy, who said he wished to visit Japan.

At a banquet in Nobuo's honor, Nobuo and Yoshi handed over the sword, which the library would display. "I never imagined I could be back in Japan alive after my flight over America," Nobuo said softly, "and I never dreamed I could visit the United States again."

Later Nobuo met one of the men who had put out his fire. "You're one of the worst fire-setters in the world," the man said. "If you're going to set another fire, do the same good job."

A local pilot flew Nobuo over the wilderness he had bombed and let him take the controls for a short while.

Before leaving America, Nobuo said that he would like to host Brookings residents in Japan one day.

That day came twenty-three years later. At Nobuo's expense, three Brookings high school students traveled to Japan. Accompanying them was the now-grown boy from the 1962 parade. For a week, Nobuo toured his guests around his country. Their goodbyes were awash with emotion. "The war is finally over for me," Nobuo said.

Nobuo made three more trips back to Brookings. At a party in 1990, he was served a large submarine sandwich topped with a plane made of sliced pickles and a half-olive helmet. Nobuo did not speak English, but everyone understood his reaction.

In 1992, one day ahead of the fiftieth anniversary of his first bombing, he planted a tree seedling at the bomb site.

In 1995, a pilot again flew him over the forest and
gave him a brief chance to fly the plane himself.

Nobuo donated thousands of dollars to the town, specifically so the library could buy children's books that celebrate other cultures. He wondered if World War II would have been different had his generation grown up reading books like those.

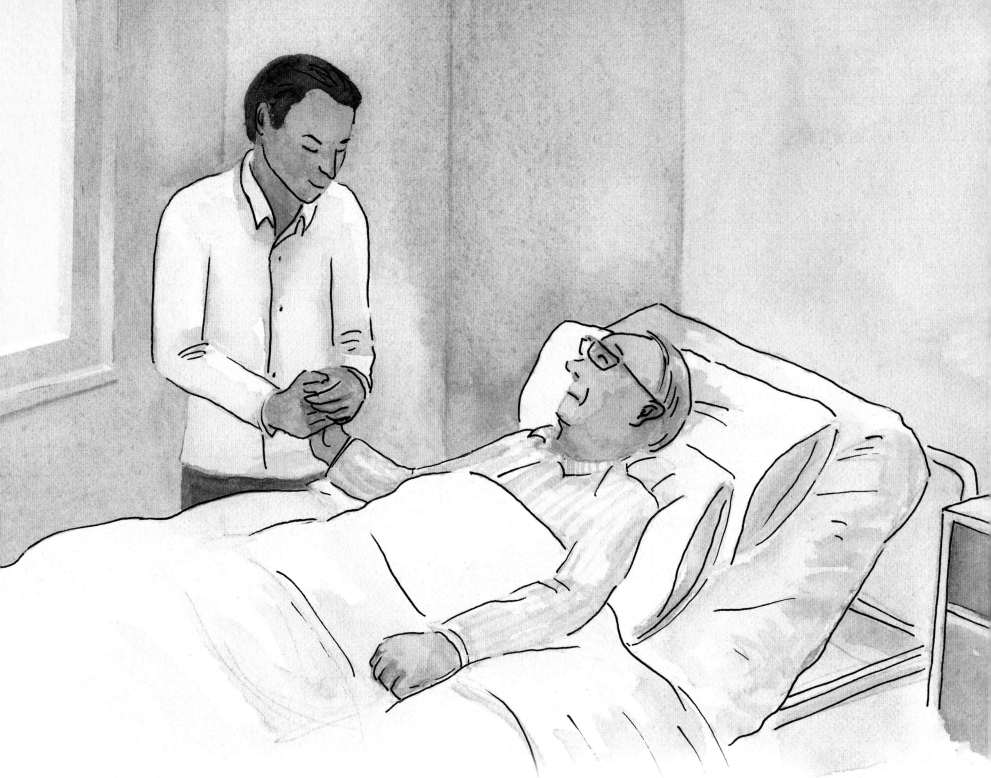

In 1997, Brookings got word that Nobuo was not well. Urgently, a town representative flew to Tokyo to tell Nobuo in person that Brookings had made him an honorary citizen, precisely fifty-five years after his second bombing.

The next day, at eighty-five, and at peace, Nobuo passed away.

The following year, as Nobuo had requested, Yoriko sprinkled some of his ashes over the bomb site. A flutist played a solo combining the national anthems of Japan and America.

At the time of his death, Nobuo was the only person who had bombed the United States mainland from a plane.

He spent much of his life hoping no one would ever take that title from him.

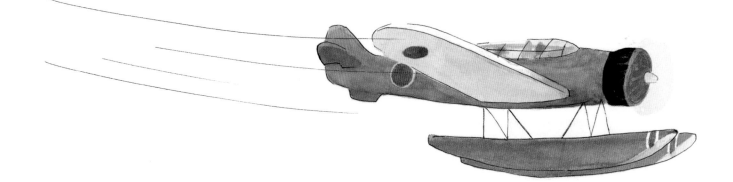

Author's Note

"What a Stupid War We Made"

If Nobuo Fujita had killed anyone in Oregon, you'd already know his name. He'd be famous in America—but not in a good way.

Nobuo's bombing run became known as the Lookout Air Raid. Though unprecedented, it did not even make him famous in Japan. He said he received no honors and no promotion. It had little effect on World War II. Yet it is one of the most thrilling and moving war stories I've heard, which is why I was compelled to write about it from the day I saw Nobuo's 1997 *New York Times* obituary. The headline called him the "only foe to bomb America."

The World War II stories we most commonly tell about the Japanese and mainland America involve one of two events. Starting in 1942, the US government forced close to 120,000 residents of Japanese descent (many of whom were American citizens) into remote internment camps—essentially prisons—in case any were spies. And in 1945, the Japanese released thousands of balloon bombs, one of which killed six people (also in Oregon). The people put into internment camps and killed by balloon bombs were civilians. They suffered as victims. Nobuo was a soldier. He suffered not because of what was done to him, but because of what he had done.

"What a stupid war we made," Nobuo said later. Though he was remorseful because of his actions, he did not pursue redemption. But when redemption pursued him—when Americans invited him to Oregon—he accepted responsibility for what he had done. He may not have been honored for attacking America, but he was honored, many times over, for apologizing to America. He went from fighting to uniting. Which took more courage?

Nobuo is not the only noble figure in this story. So were the people of Brookings and the people of America who supported the idea of a visit from Nobuo despite the often-heated opposition. One of those supporters said, "Surely after twenty years, bitterness should be over and acts of bravery, no matter by whom, commended." Oregon governor Mark O. Hatfield said, "If we who fought the Japanese are able to forgive, then I trust those few who have protested will reconsider."

Nobuo almost didn't survive the war, in which case there would have been no chance to reconcile. In August 1945, he was ordered to fly a kamikaze mission, destroying an enemy ship by crashing his plane into it, which would have killed him too.

But five days before the mission, the war ended. His life spared, Nobuo was free to embark on his next and final mission: promoting peace.

Selected Sources

Bowers, Everett P. *Military History*. "Aerial Attack on Oregon." June 2000.

Corvallis Gazette-Times. "Give Us the Truth on the War." September 21, 1942.

Deatherage, Curt. *The Creswell Chronicle*. "Bombs Over Brookings." February 21, 2007.

Hansen, Sue. *World War II*. "A pair of Japanese bombs dropped on an Oregon forest furthered the cause of international peace." September 1997.

Hoff, Derek. *Public Historian, The*, volume 21, number 2. "Igniting Memory: Commemoration of the 1942 Japanese Bombing of Southern Oregon, 1962–1998." Spring 1999.

Horn, Steve. *The Second Attack on Pearl Harbor: Operation K and Other Japanese Attempts to Bomb America in World War II*. Naval Institute Press, 2005.

Japan Times Weekly. "One Man's War: 1942 air raid leads to 1985 friendship." August 10, 1985.

Langenberg, William H. *Aviation History*. "Japanese Bomb the Continental U.S. West Coast." November 1998.

Life on the Home Front: Oregon Responds to WWII. "Bombs Fall on Oregon: Japanese Attacks on the State." http://sos.oregon.gov/archives/exhibits/ww2/Pages/threats-bombs.aspx.

Los Angeles Times. "Jap Incendiary Sets Forest Fire." http://gesswhoto.com/oregon-bombing.html. September 15, 1942.

McCash, William. *Bombs Over Brookings*. self-published, 2005.

New York Times. Kristof, Nicholas D. "Nobuo Fujita, 85, Is Dead; Only Foe to Bomb America." October 3, 1997.

Oregon Journal. "Curry County Gets First Jap Bomb to Fall in Continental U.S." September 15, 1942.

Oregonian, The. "I Bombed the U.S.A.," U.S. Naval Institute Proceedings, by Nobuo Fujita, formerly Warrant Flying Officer, Imperial Japanese Navy, and Chief Journalist Joseph D. Harrington, U.S. Navy, June 1961; reprinted in June 18, 1961.

Sullivan, William L. *Hiking Oregon's History: The Stories Behind Historic Places You Can Walk to See*. Navillus Press, 2003.

Time. "Oregon: Raider's Return." May 25, 1962.

Webber, Burt and Margie. *Fujita, Flying Samurai*. Self-published, 2000.

Woodbury, Chuck. *Out West*, issue 11. "World War II air raid of Oregon was a real bomb!" July 1990.

All dialogue is excerpted from published articles and interviews.